Things I Will Put in My Mother's Pocket

Catherine Graham

Indigo Dreams Publishing

First Edition: Things I Will Put In My Mother's Pocket
First published in Great Britain in 2013 by:
Indigo Dreams Publishing
132 Hinckley Road
Stoney Stanton
Leics
LE9 4LN

www.indigodreams.co.uk

Catherine Graham has asserted her right under the Copyright, Designs and Patents Act 1988 to be identified as the author of this work.
© 2013 Catherine Graham

ISBN 978-1-909357-08-2

British Library Cataloguing in Publication Data. A CIP record for this book can be obtained from the British Library.

Designed and typeset in Palatino Linotype by Indigo Dreams.

Cover design by Ronnie Goodyer
Author photograph © picturesbybish (Chris Bishop)
Printed and bound in Great Britain by Imprint Academic, Exeter.

Papers used by Indigo Dreams are recyclable products made from wood grown in sustainable forests following the guidance of the Forest Stewardship Council.

*With love to my mother and late father
and to my late sister, Sandra*

Some of these poems or versions of them have previously appeared in the following publications: *Reach Poetry*, *The New Writer*, *Pulsar*, *Other Poetry*, *Citylife*, *The Stony Thursday Book*, (New Series No.8) ed. Ciaran O'Driscoll (Arts Office of Limerick County Council, Ireland, 2009), *Two Rivers Meet*, ed. Dominic Taylor/Keith Armstrong, (Revival Press, Ireland/Northern Voices, England 2008), *Crablines Off The Pier*, ed. Ronnie Goodyer/Dawn Bauling (Indigo Dreams Publishing, 2010), *Still The Sea Rolls On*, ed. Keith Armstrong/Peter Dixon (North Tyneside Council/ Northern Voices, 2012), *Gaps In The Sequence*, ed. Lisa Matthews (The Stemistry Project, 2009), *9 til 5*, ed. Sheree Mack (ID on Tyne Press 2008), *Book of Ten*, ed. Jeff Price/Annie Moir (Zebra Publishing 2009), *The Pink Lane Poetry Book*, ed. Jessica Johnson/Bish (Pink Lane/picturesbybish Publishing, 2010), *Soul Feathers*, ed. Ronnie Goodyer/Annie Morgan (Indigo Dreams Publishing, 2011) in aid of Macmillan Cancer Support, *Poetry Kite* (online), *Caught In The Net* (online), *Transparent Words* (online), *Poetry Tyneside* (online), *Diamond Twig* (online), 3LIGHTS (online) *A Night at the Movies*, ed. Jim Bennett (ebook, Poetry Kit, 2012).

A selection of these poems also appeared in the chapbook *Signs* (ID on Tyne Press, 2010).

Daughters of Tyne forms part of the collaborative poem *Echoes of The Tyne* written with Sheree Mack and Wajid Hussain and is taken from the anthology *Proud To Call It Home, Newcastles of the World*, (ID on Tyne Press, 2012). *Northern Vowels* forms part of the collaborative poem, *Highway Headed South* with Lynn Ciesielski (USA) and Lesley Burt (UK).

Some of these poems have been broadcast on NE1 Radio, some have been recorded at www.listenupnorth.com

Also by Catherine Graham

Signs (ID on Tyne Press, 2010)

CONTENTS

Things I Will Put In My Mother's Pocket

Making Marmalade With Marc Bolan

Riding a white swan
cannot compare with the joy of
making marmalade with Marc Bolan.
His hands, so skilful
he could peel an orange in his back pocket.
Peeling oranges
as if undressing a princess,
a diva, a whore,
before bringing the fruit gently to the boil:
Simmering
like a secret; biting her tongue,
bittersweet.

Delicious, irresistible: spread generously
at breakfast, like glittering gold leaf.

Signs

When I set out on my journey
I shall leave home early.

I shall wear shoes that breathe slowly;
button up my best coat.

My scarf will wrap itself around me,
brushing my cheek like a newborn hand

and I shall need a bag, the one
that smells of her favourite perfume.

A simple sign
nailed to a wooden post.

See her alight with only the ghost
of a well dressed smile.

This is the place
where dandelion clocks stand still.

I'm Not Struck On Her Upstairs

She has loud sex.
Passes me on the stairs,
her and her Waitrose carrier bags.
All skimmed milk
and muesli,
you know the sort.
Only smiles with her face.

Them downstairs think she's great
but I have to listen to her
panting like an Olympian,
hitting notes like a sex-crazed soprano.
I turn up my radio:
tune in to Night Owls.

Her man wants a medal like a frying pan
for putting up with all that grief.
Him with his voice like velvet.
His eyes like Omar Sharif.

She Wishes For A Poem By Yuri Zhivago

Write me a poem Yuri, like the ones you wrote for Lara.
She doesn't deserve them, she swanned off with Kamarovsky.
I pity you, torn between her and Tonya.

Poor Yuri the poetic doctor, left to tend to Lara's mother.
So tell me: your poems, I bet they rhyme flawlessly.
Write me a poem Yuri, like the ones you wrote for Lara.

She had you, Kamarovsky and then there was Pasha!
Seems to me like she lived life horizontally.
I pity you, torn between her and Tonya.

Is it the angelic look, tell me, what is it about her
that compels you to write love poems endlessly?
Write me a poem Yuri, like the ones you wrote for Lara.

I love the scene where she rests her head on your shoulder.
(I've never read the book, I've only seen the movie.)
I pity you, torn between her and Tonya.

Oh I could look into your dark eyes forever
and what I would give to read how much you love *me*.
Write me a poem Yuri, like the ones you wrote for Lara.
I pity you, torn between her and Tonya.

Making Clogs At Gallowgate
for Doris

I let him believe I'm fourteen; old enough
to be a clog-maker. The rough, green overall
tied tight around my waist gives me the figure
I haven't got: I comb my fringe to the side.
Uppers hang in the workshop like kippers;
the genuine smell of leather all around.
Gripping the sycamore sole between my legs,
I squeeze my knees together, like mam
says I always should, and hammer like hell
at the horseshoe, braying the nails into the wood:
slicing leather with the sharpest knife in the world;
my hands bleeding, like Christ up on the cross.
Soon I'll be promoted to stretching the skins
over metal lasts, if I keep my head down.
My workmates are five sisters, all would-be
opera singers. Listen, you can hear them
even now, *Si tu ne m'aimes pas prends garde à toi!*
And old Ebenezer next door, stitching:
our would-be baritone. Every morning
we're greeted by a longtail that runs along the pipes.
The same R.A.T. (for it's unlucky to say the word),
comes out again at noon, scurrying around
like a frantic clerk of works, on the look out
for idle crumbs. The loud clock ticka ticka ticka ticks
its way to Friday when the shop window's filled
with beautiful black clogs, perched in pairs
on shelves, like lovebirds, and I collect my
seven and six. That's when I leave work
by the front door, so I can pass the window
and Fenwick's with its felt hats and blouses
made from the finest of satins and silks.

Hyem
Home

She welcomes with a smile as wide as the Tyne.
This city celebrates different voices.

Her daughters sold clothes, second-hand at Sandgate
as the boats sailed like long lost lovers into Dean Street,
keeping their promise.

Reborn, her lassie sings a brand new song,
silencing the battalion of buses
that bully past the building societies,

while the lads that once danced for their daddies
push bairns in buggies, with one hand.

And still, people remain puddled
by the play of her spirited, underground rivers
that flow, like lifeblood right up to Spital Tongues.

She is a carnival of bridges skinning a heron-coloured sky.
Flooded with pride, she lands her logo
like kisses, on lamp posts in Grey Street.

Daughters Of Tyne

I

Martha's neddin cake rests
like a full moon on the scullery workbench,

the smell of warm dough
wafting along the passage to the end room

where Nancy keeps her savings
in a yellow-white chest of drawers.

She has no idea that every Monday,
my mother borrows a pound note,

promising herself she'll replace it by Friday,
before Nancy clocks off at the liver salts factory.

Many a time it's a photo finish between Nancy
getting off the bus and mam replacing the note.

By October, mother permitting,
there'll be enough for the wedding.

II

Edie has never married, never met
the man of her dreams, a man who

plays for United and bleeds black
and white. He has a quiff like Elvis

and a voice like Pat Boon; smokes filter tip
cigarettes. He is as hard as December

and gentle as July, slightly bow-legged
with a glint in his eye like Russ Conway.

If ever he swears he puts tuppence in the cuss box.
Romance is played down for love is

carrying the coal up three flights of stairs.
There will be two children, a boy

who can kick a ball like his father
and a girl who can kick even higher.

III

The women I grew up with had
tell it like it is voices. They favoured vowels,

vowels that flex mouths
like opera singers limbering up for an aria.

They made soup from bones and knitted
anything from booties to balaclavas.

Bless them, for they breastfed their babies
and had bairns vaccinated via sugar cubes.

The women I knew made their feelings known
in a clash of pans. Always there

at the school gates, their headscarves
blowing like flags in the biting north-easterly wind.

They believed in the Bible and best butter
and knew by heart, their Co-op dividend number.

Sister

I tell her
how scared I am of clowns and the night
then snuggle up beside her, safe.

We giggle
about things girls shouldn't do
on a first date.

In my 'in love' years, she's wise:
'Here, wipe your nose,
fish in the sea and all that.'

There are days
when we argue over unimportant things
and she turns up the volume.

My shoes are in neat pairs under the bed:
her books are strewn across the floor.
People tell me we were very different

and as a child I never asked why
mam would tear March out of every calendar,
she still circles every 16th July.

Only Child

The only child cannot come home late
unnoticed
or win pillow fights.

They don't know how it feels
to share a sister's secret,

they don't have older brothers
to blacken a bully's eye.

Do not envy the only child.
They must wait
for elderly relatives to play a board game.

They learn too late
that love doesn't always come easy.

The only child is the apple
of their parents' hopeful eye.

The Hoppings Comes To Town Moor

We set off straight after school:
four aunts, mam and a tank of a woman
who called herself Aunty Mary. I preferred to
stay close to Aunt Edie, unmarried and working
at the Co-op. A razzmatazz of lightbulbs flashed
around the moor like a painfree migraine.
As the music grew louder we could see masses
of Lowry people all heading for the rides.
Chart-topping records invited us to join the party:
Del Shannon, Brenda Lee and Elvis, Aunt Edie *loved* Elvis.
As if battery operated, two aunts began to bop.
Overcome by a warm cowpat, they stopped
and nipped their noses like synchronised swimmers.
Scarier than the Ghost Train, the sight of *Aunty Mary*
in the Hall of Mirrors was bewildering. Of course,
I wasn't allowed to ride anything dangerous
but the excitement of prize bingo was infectious.
Aunt Martha hooked a duck; mam complained
about the lack of decent coconuts and we all took a shine
to the goldfish with black spots. We called it Billy
after Billy the Fish, da's best pal at The Black Bull.
Emerging from the fortune teller's moonlit caravan,
Aunt Edie suggested it was time to leave,
Rosa Lee had obviously read the wrong script.
All the way home, Aunt Edie hummed that song from G.I. Blues.
I could have told her, marrying Elvis was never on the cards.

Threads

I used to pray that I'd wake up right-handed.
This I believed, would make her like me.

I remember how she would draw a deep breath,
eyes in ecstasy as nimble-fingered girls

presented their embroidery, then a sideways glance
and like a suspicious bird she would glare at me,

pecking away at any confidence I'd mustered
from craft books at the library. She was the reason

I stayed home dodging the school board man,
special agent X with his briefcase and trilby.

I knew his knock, his five syllable voice,
'Open the door now.' 'I know you are in.' Sometimes

he would try to force a note through the letter box
but I was wise to what his envelope would contain:

Dear Mrs. B, I am very concerned about your daughter's absence.
You really must try to improve her attendance. I did go back

eventually. She and her teacher friend laughed at me,
told me I was a wimp for taking her too seriously.

I often wonder if she saw me as the price she had to pay
for working in the inner city. I saw *her* as the class bully.

I Beg To Apply For The Post
after Jack Common, 1903 - 1968

My school was tough:
the teachers weighed in,
tipping the scales with their red pencils,
their toxic, chalk dust.
I beg to apply for the post.

Like you, my father learned shorthand;
attended evening class at the colliery.
A cacophony of skills, don't you think?
Like my mother, singing opera in the scullery.
Beware of the man who wants marriage,
isn't that what you told your readers?
My father taught me to ride a bike
and not depend on stabilizers.
He hated smarmy men the most.
I beg to apply for the post.

No silver spoons in our house.
Our doorstep was donkey stoned.
We refused to be shoved into snobbery,
refused to give up the ghost
when they refurbished The Dwellings
and named it Millennium Court.
Ashes to ashes, communities to dust.
I beg to apply for the post.

I've never failed to fit in,
never lived in a 'culture vacuum'.
Why, our back lane was a canvas
to the local graffiti artist.
I beg to apply for the post.

Brought up on Dickman's pies
but I never mince my words.
I don't give anything I don't want to.
I don't go about hard-faced.
I'm not fighting any class war
in silk lined, kid gloves:
I have a voice, I haven't lost faith.
I'm taking on life bare knuckled,
this kiddar's luck has changed.

I don't believe in the twaddle
I read in most of the papers.
I know when to tell the truth;
when to spout the necessary lie.
I learned all this at my cost,
I beg to apply for the post.

I would supply references
from my previous employer
though, fair to say there was no love lost.
He had ideas above my station,
his wife was all fur coat.
More edge than a broken piss pot.
I beg to apply for the post.

I pride myself on being punctual,
always on the dot.
I don't pretend or hope to be
what I'm definitely not.
I tick all of the boxes,
I call salmon pâté, salmon paste.
I know my place but I don't like to boast.
I beg to apply for the post.

Bread

A homeless man sits hand out
on the church steps.

Three hatted women,
freshly blessed and clean

stand over him like an agony of aunts.
The man gets up and moves on,

his pockets empty, like yesterday
when he sat next to a cash machine.

When The Ship Sails Up Dean Street

Weapons will melt
like winter snow
and we'll wake up

Singing.

Rain will remember
to fall on Africa
and we'll bring in the crops

Dancing.

Rivers will rush
to meet sapphire seas
and the polluters will say
'We're sorry.'

Wishing.

Doorways will offer
a welcome
and not just a cardboard box.

Caring.

Food will be spread
across the world's table
and we'll take just what we need.

Sharing.

Peacemakers will
persuade politicians
to hear what they have to say.

Listening.

And we'll echo the dream
for tomorrow,
but *we'd* help it happen today.

Talking.

Heading For Albert Dock, Liverpool 2011

Darlington to Northallerton
had taken way too long, car sick
we passed the turn off for Leeds.

Even the satnav, Stella, sighed
as she reported more road works.
'We are calculating a new route.'

New route? New route?
We've been on the road
for how many hours? And you're

calculating a new route?
How many 'new routes' can there be
from Newcastle to bloody Liverpool?

All my life I've wanted to visit
The Beatles museum, well since I was
just seventeen, you know what I mean?

And all that's coming between
me and my dream is butter wouldn't melt
between her legs Stella, telling me she's

'calculating a new route'.
When I get there, I'll wear
my John Lennon tee shirt, the one
with lyrics and stars printed on the back.

On Arriving In Albert Dock, Liverpool 2011

The hotel, once a warehouse, welcomed us
as if we were rich. Charmed by the receptionist,
like a virgin I blushed and confessed

it was my first time in Liverpool,
its river, louder, wider than mine.
Voices from the north, further north and south

Babel'd the lobby. A clued up woman
sitting like the Lorelei on a pile of suitcases,
pencilled a crossword, murmuring answers to herself.

The mystery tour from home to here was
well worth the diversions I thought, as we lugged ourselves
up the stairs. Our room's view didn't disappoint:

on one side the Mersey, on the other The Beatles Story
and below, in the rain, a dead ringer for John.

Poem For John Lennon

Where do I begin?

Isn't that a line from Love Story? Can't you come up with
an original line for my bloody poem?

So where do I begin to write a poem about
John Winston Ono Lennon?
Is it true that bombs were falling even as you were being born?
Oxford Street Maternity Hospital 1940, Liverpool.

This isn't going to be some sentimental timeline, is it?
Some kind of spot the song title crap.
You shouldn't write to impress,
you shouldn't seek anyone's approval.
You're not picking a career, you're just writing a bloody poem.

I'm not out to impress, I just want to do you proud.
I'm working class, you're my hero for crying out loud.

Writing to impress is like entering a Leek Show competition.
You work away on your best produce,
hoping to grow the biggest and best poem. Best in Bloom
taking the Blue Ribbon: taking the piss more like.

I'll write that you are the man who
made world leaders lose their sleep,
made dreamers sit up and listen.
I'll keep my poem simple,
keep you safe in my down-to-earth ink.
I'll write about the Bed-ins, your non-violent protest.
The press, minus sense of humour,
didn't get it and hovered around you, like gannets.

My friend Viv and I sing your songs all the time,
we love the ones you penned just for the people.
At the risk of sounding dead sugary,
you were always our favourite Beatle.

That line's got more sugar than strawberry jam.

Or Strawberry Fields?

Just write the bloody poem.

Love and light, John. Love and light.

Rock and Roll, Kid. Rock and Roll.
You've got some front for a working class poet.
Mind you don't find yourself living on the hill.

The Apprentice

Three builders sit at their favourite table.
Behind them, the bar, hexagonal. Lit up
like a U.F.O. On display, a bevy of

sapphire, emerald and amber bottles:
a chorus line of optics to tempt the most
committed teetotal. Looking more than

ready to order, the builders check the board
for Friday's special offer: *Beef and ale pie,*
scampi or *chicken tikka masala.*

Still in their work gear, black tee shirts and
overalls splattered with plaster, attention
turns to page three of the apprentice's

morning paper. 'Fancy that?' they tease
and ruffle his boy band hair. The lad
tells them to get lost and folds his paper

for later. All three look up from their plates
as two scantily dressed women high heel
their way past the bar. The blonde catwalks

to the toilet, her friend follows behind
like a maid of honour. 'Fancy that?'
the grinning apprentice asks the gaffer.

'Just finish your scampi,' the gaffer grunts.
'You've got a blocked U-bend to sort
in less than half an hour. Any questions,

you're sorry you're late, you had to deal with
an emergency call, you got held up
on the motorway, road works on the A1.'

Blossom
Daniel O'Donnell fan

Toe-tapping in time,
lost in da's tired, tartan slippers
that rise and fall like shuggy boats,
her small purple feet swing to and fro,
she's watching a Daniel video.
Singing only special words out loud,
she picks out Daniel's sisters in the audience.
'The dark one's a singer as well.'
She tells me, as if she's well in.
Her catalogue skirt hangs
like a perfectly drawn royal blue curtain,
box pleated over her bounce the baby knees.
Still, as she leans forward to turn up the volume,
I catch sight of the aspirin that passes for a popper
in one of her suspenders, clinging vice-like
to her stocking in its game of tug of war.
I see her hands held as if in prayer,
her vapour rubbing, soothing, loving hands,
plump like warm, unbaked bread: stottie cakes.
She catches me looking at her
when my eyes should be on Daniel.
Her eyes, as blue as the engagement ring
she never would ask for,
for in all the years she shared with my father,
material things were the last thing on her mind.
Shh, he's singing her favourite song.
Once more, in the three o'clock sunlight,
her Anne Shelton hair shines like the yellow silk blouse
she would borrow for The Brighton;
dancing the last dance with her beloved Bill
before sharing a bag of chips on the way home, smiling.

Things I Will Put In My Mother's Pocket

The photograph taken
on the veranda,
his arm around her shoulder.

The letter he sent
from Yeovil.
Her first-born's silver bangle.

Imperial Leather soap,
a comb
and a clean apron.

A Jim Reeves L.P.,
a bottle of
Youth Dew perfume.

The way he'd call her bonnie lass
and touch her cheek
as she entered the room.

Three rings
I'll not answer,
letting me know she's safe home.

She Loves Having A Poem On The Go

She loves having a poem on the go,
just as Martha loved
having some knitting on the go.

The click clack of consonants,
the plain and purl of images looped together.

With every vowel, every syllable speaking volumes,
the poem begins to take shape.

Though reluctant to cast off and start a new one,
she wears her latest poem like a favourite cardigan,
unbuttoned, comfortable, on the face of it.

The Fever Van
after the painting by L. S. Lowry, 1935

Some poor sod must be sick.
Not surprising
given the smog and the smoke.
Lungs like empty coal sacks,

empty bar the dust.
Neighbours gather at the goings on:
some crane their necks,
some look side-eyed

as pittle-coloured disinfectant
drip drip drips from a doorstep.
Chances are
it's one of Mary Skidmore's lads;

heard him coughing his guts up
when I called for the rent.
She asked me to call back tomorrow,
she knows and I know it's been spent.

Squandered away at the bookies,
ten bob says I'm right. Trust me,
I know Tom Skidmore,
blown his entire pay packet I'll bet.

Please God it's not their only daughter,
the lass can only be nine.
Her smile the spit of her mother;
face like a porcelain doll.

The van door's flung open,
a mother mouthes a familiar prayer,
'Suffer little children ...'
Looks like another safe bet.

Industrial Panorama

after the painting by L. S. Lowry, 1953

A blackened church corners the red brick terrace,
its priestly tall steeple poking a fag end sky
and in pews as straight as rolling pins, lean parishioners

pray for score draws, best butter and *Bless me Father*,
the odd pint and a packet of Woodbines.
Look closely at the foot of the darkest hill,

there's a game going on that has the lane creased
with laughter: *Keep in, keep in wherever you are,
the cats and dogs are at your door!*

The hide and seek chant echoes across the terraces,
like match day, when flat-capped men find their voices.
Is that a monument, a mausoleum to the right of

the seven deadly smokestacks?
The burial place perhaps of the fat factory owner:
May he rest in peace, may the women at least

have something decent or otherwise to discuss
on the street; headscarved and slippered at back doors.
A full bodied dog in the foreground barks

at street lamps that hang their heads
while telegraph poles stand proud as Punch,
firing messages to *suits* who share their beds

with polished, well coiffed wives,
not necessarily their own, according to the local chinwag
who does a bit of cleaning on the side.

Pay day can't come quick enough, she coughs up
and pays her bills, dreaming of the day when
she'll make ends meet and see past these satanic hills.

Maybe one day her ship will come in
and she'll slap a deposit down, for if there's sunlight,
it remains well hidden in this smokescreened, treeless town.

Seeing The Whole Picture

after The Great Wave, Katsushika Hokusai c. 1830

A novel way to spend Saturday morning,
a free talk by a Friend of the Gallery.

Had it been a good drying day,
the bed clothes would have taken priority.

The Friend, she decided, was a retired teacher,
all pencil and tapping foot.

There are bound to be questions later
she thought, so she took down copious notes.

Making all the right noises in all the right places
like the crowd in The Emperor's New Clothes,

she wowed at the blues in the seascape
but she still couldn't see the boats.

How To Suss Out The Night Staff
Ward 1

Do not ask anyone
who only smiles with their face:
They are on auto pilot.

When you need iced water in the night,
ask the one who sings
Beach Boys songs to herself in the kitchen.

Join in:
Bar Bar Bar Bar Barbara Ann

Harmonise:
Bar Bar Bar Bar Barbara Ann

Then, for you are now best friends:
'Any chance of a top-up?'

Rockin' and a reelin' Barbara Ann
Bar Bar Bar Barbara Ann.

Dancing With Angels

'Is she usually like this?'
the nurse asks indifferently.

No, she's not usually a ballerina,
I've never heard her sing like this, beautiful, carefree.

Perhaps I am meeting her for the first time,
perhaps *this* is how she wants to be,

free from all our expectations, skimming stones
across reality. I want to congratulate her,

be her first and last dancing partner
for I know in this blue moon moment

that soon her parade will be over.
I lie beside her, listening

to breathless conversations with her sisters
who step from a sepia photograph

as the room whispers the scent
of invisible flowers.

I watch as her fingers grow long,
her fingertips, turquoise, cold.

On her lips a silent song,
trials, like rocks spilling out from her pillow.

Ukulele Nights At The Cumberland Arms, Byker

Coats pile up in the corner
as regulars take their seats
in the small dusty lounge, ukuleles

like newborn babies in their arms.
No need to audition, show off
or ask permission, anyone can

take the lead with a song. First up,
a woman strums *Have I told you lately?*
then switches to *Your cheatin' heart*

and as if on football terraces,
everyone knows the words.
A young man takes up the challenge

to play something by The Beatles.
He puts his glass down and plays
like he's blessed with extra fingers.

The room is a concert arena,
onlookers clap their hands sore.
Some knock on tables as in dominoes

and smokers outside join the applause.
Poets hover on their way upstairs
to the monthly open mic

as Leonard Cohen fans strum *Hallelujah*
like they do every ukulele night.
Meanwhile, propped up at the bar,

an old soldier serenades a ghost.
Albert licks his lips
and slurs a tipsy *Are you lonesome tonight?*

Black Bullets And Vinegar

The wind, the wind, the wind blows high,
in comes her sweetheart from the sky.

The old washing line is a skipping rope
for girls who giggle as the wind blows high.
Inside, a remedy for chestiness
stands in the oven, over the coal fire.
Black bullets and vinegar, brown sugar
to sweeten: a linctus to be swallowed
like lies. The aftertaste hangs in my mouth;
lingers on my tongue like grief, bittersweet.

I return the photograph to the tin
and whisper low for only her to hear.
Make me a cure, grandma, to take away
this pain: make me a girl again. I'll take
any remedy. Leave it in the press,
your magic cupboard with frosted glass doors.

Losing Stripes
for W.B.

Perhaps
it was the tune that was playing,
rippling across the fields from the dance hall.

Or a letter he'd opened
that morning
with its whisper of Coty perfume

that persuaded him
to pity his young prisoner
and allow them to meet at the gates.

Whatever the war-torn reason,
he told him to hold her close.
The darkest sun

will burn more brightly
every time you close your eyes
and see her face.

Cutting My Father's Hair

It was the summer of K-tel LPs, compilation albums
of favourite vocalists. With my father at forty-two
and myself six months shy of fifteen, I prayed that

a haircut might be the answer. My father, in his
frayed green shirt and sweep-black cords, sat
motionless on the kitchen chair as in a life drawing class,

his world-weary hands resting on his lap, brown
brogues fixed firmly to the floor, a gift to any artist.
Pages from the Evening Chronicle lay like a hand of cards

on the lino: *Births, Deaths* and *Marriages*. Happy couples
posing for the camera as wisps of black hair drifted
like confetti to the floor, the snip snip of my scissors

piercing the silence. Salon-like I held up the mirror,
'Going somewhere special Sir?' Still in salon mode
I moved from side to side allowing my client full view of

my handiwork. My father smiled. I looked in on him
later. Doing my best not to disturb his light sleep, I left
a kiss on his brow. 'Tomorrow I'll fetch you the moon,'

I whispered, before noticing the mirror, abandoned, face down.

Watch Light

Watching him at the computer: he has my father's hands.
Long-fingered
he brushes the bloodless, grey keyboard,
talking in caps lock: the tongue of newfangled technology.

Once more, through gauzy half-light, my father's hands
carry the old wooden wireless into the kitchen,

its brassy sound box, oval
like a brooch that an aunt would wear.

It must be Saturday,
someone is reading requests for favourite listeners.

Mountain-high on his shoulders,
I'm skimming invisible stones,
near grazing the leafy crowns of spirited trees.

Reaching out
my fingers sieve the scented droplets of a summer rain shower,
as if playing some unseen squeeze box.

July, 1969.
The swinging transistor spits;
splutters in its butter-coloured carrying case.

And it's down five places to number nine!
The dimpled DJ tells his faithful *Pop Pickers*
who tune in at the tea table.

There's a brave boy knocking at the back door:
One small step for man.

Moon landing. Earth moving?
Is paradise half as nice and is sixteen ever sweet?

Lovingly he touches my mother's cheek.
Saying nothing. Saying everything.

Spring, 1982
In my eye, veiled music.
And sons are fighting for Goose Green.

26th July 1982, my father's hands, cold. Still.

Seen From Above

after Louis Macneice

Tiny black trees
make newsprint of the snow.
Snowballs fly
back and forth across the lake
like an early games console.

Footprints
spoil the icing sugar path
as a park keeper points
his metronome finger.

Children's laughter drowns
the music of swans.

The Agoraphobic Poet Sends Her Shoes
With A Covering Letter To The Local Cobbler

As per our telephone conversation:
Here are the shoes, can you do anything with them?

They don't seem to want to go out. They've been looking
a little down at heel and now it's come about that they've been
making up excuses to avoid leaving the house. They won't
tell me the problem, they just refuse to step outside. They tell me
they'll go out 'tomorrow', I think they're taking me for a ride
because tomorrows come and go and still, I'm stuck inside.

No amount of love or gentle persuasion can make them change
their mind. I've tried telling them to relax, take deep breaths and
focus: it's as if someone's cast a spell on them, some kind of
hocus-pocus. So I was wondering if you might fix them or are
they beyond repair? I'd be much obliged if you could mend them
or make me another pair that will want to go out walking,
the way *we* used to do.

I've enclosed the cost of return postage,
I'm very grateful to you.

Letter To Steve Wright's Sunday Lovesongs

Dear Steve,

Would you please play a request for my husband Roger
who has given me the best year of my life. Roger left me
twelve months ago for someone younger. He told me
how he felt alive again when she walked into the office and
typed her way into his life. I bet he sat up like a meerkat and
couldn't believe his luck when she stroked his hair and
whispered, 'Fancy taking me for a drink?'

Please play something appropriate and remind him
he was no great shakes. All that puffing and panting that
went on between the sheets was merely chronic asthma, the sex
was mediocre. How about Jerry Lee Lewis? Or, would it be
insensitive to request The Beatles, *When I'm Sixty-four*?

Roger always dreaded getting older and losing his hair,
I can fully understand why he thought that shagging the lovely
Claire might stop the ageing process right there in its tracks.
Bless. The only thing she stopped was *him* wearing nylon
underpants.

He's a huge Elvis fan so might I suggest *Blue Suede Shoes*?
I can't deny I was devastated last week when I heard the news
that Roger has lost his job. Caught in a cupboard apparently
by his newly appointed boss who accepted Claire's explanation
that she was on her knees looking for a lens. He told her to
wipe her pretty face; that she could always 'make amends'.

So I'd like to send best wishes to Roger and Claire,
the happy couple. Tell him it takes more than cod liver oil to
keep a relationship supple. Tell him that I've moved on, that I too
have met someone new. We're looking forward to
wearing purple and making plans together. She reminds me I'm
still beautiful as she smiles at me in the mirror.

Waiting For The Orgasmobile To Come
A song to Love, 2058

Surely there is more to life than
cowboy stem cell banks.

Romance, gone.
The drugs drop lads moved on
to back street deals in Orgasmobiles.

Step into the back of the motor,
Button A gets you a son
Button B gets you a daughter.

Button C gets you a high
then leaves you wondering why
love is against the law.

No one says *I love you*
or whispers, *You're the one.* Just
Press Button B for a daughter.
Press Button A for a son.

The Librarian

You tell me I look like a librarian:
the grey and black, the lack

of mascara. So what does a librarian
look like in your book? Tell me,

where do you get the notion that
librarians are minus emotion?

Perhaps it's you who needs a stroll
down the self help section. See,

this wordsmith loves thrillers
and erotic fiction. So don't be

deceived by the flat shoes
and roll neck sweater. Don't knock

what you haven't undressed
and never judge a poet by her cover.

The Pitman Poet

Joseph Skipsey 1832 - 1903

No light, bonny lad, bar the odd candle end.
A trapper at seven years,
opening and closing, opening and closing the dusty door

from dawn to sunset, lending ventilation
to the hell hole of the pit.

Tracing your finger in coal dust
you taught yourself to write:
copying handbills, passing endless black hours

before climbing the mine owner's rusted ladder
to home and a bowl of nettle broth. Eight bairns to feed,
her man shot dead; your mother, the love of his life.

Who would believe that you would grow up to quote
Shakespeare and Burns; to write poems from coal,
poems that endure like diamonds.

204 Men And Boys
Hartley Pit Disaster 16th January 1862

I'd swear I saw him in the street,
I swear I heard him singing
for he always had a canny voice,
a gift in such a young 'un.

Don't tell me
he's not singing now, hoying stones
from them damn wagons.
And I'll not believe he'll not answer
to any of his names

for he'd surely answer to his ma
with a line from our special song,
the song I'd sing him to sleep with
from being a babby in my arms.

I thank people for their kindness
and I'm glad his faather held him
and I cannot help but wonder
if it was that song he wad be singing,
for as sure as curse'd coal is black
the bairn would sing his young heart out.

Singing 'til they all fell asleep,
one by one, never to waken.

Promise
i.m. Jane Anderson

When the moon clocks on tonight
we'll paint Darn Crook
in shades of favourite roses,

wear pink slip-ons
and hit a dozen dance floors.
If there's a dress code we'll crack it in style.

We'll push the boat out
and sail up Grey Street,
knowing you'd approve this celebration.

Our way
of keeping a promise
while you bloom in a different season.

We'll sing to your favourite tune.
If there are tears
we'll sing out louder.

And when stars do their best
to outshine you
and rain clouds try to spoil our parade

we'll link arms
and kick like showgirls,
blow a thousand kisses into the sky.

Torn

You pass the folded page to me,
a jagged edge down one side where

you've torn it from a magazine:
some of your favourite poetry.

I read the poems
then read again more closely.

No love lines, there doesn't need to be.
Enough that you had thought of me.

Souvenir

Flashbacks
polished like prized bric-a-brac.

The lustre of love
longed for like sleep, sleep
for the insomniac.

When do memories become souvenirs,
trophies
tarnished by quicksilver tears?

If, when all is said
and inevitably done,
we pay the piper, we call the tune

then it's the pure gold shine of your love
I'll remember;
your mouth, your kiss, your atomic number.

Sticks And Stones

Even though you beat me,
you cannot keep me under your table.

You beat me
to put me in my right place
as a woman. My right place is being free.

Free to fight for the right to speak out.
Speak out against injustice, inaction, poverty.

If you believe that pain will
make me put my hands over my mouth,
then you are misled.

I cup my hands up to my lips and drink
to Justice, Equality, Dignity.

For I do not fade like a bruise fades,
I heal like a broken bone.

Extract Taken From Poetry And The Menopause

Out of one hundred women in the 45 to 50 age range, 89 have reported hot flushes redder than a Donegal sunset, heartbeats like heels on a Kerry dance floor whilst listening to a daring new CD featuring poetry from some of Ireland's best known voices. One woman, who wished to remain nameless, came close to tears as she confessed to speeding on the A1. 'I guess I was doing around 90,' she admitted to flush researcher Dr. Dan Madra. 'I was listening to track 11 when my vision became blurred, I didn't know if I was coming or going. I looked in my mirror and was startled by the play of my eyeballs rolling in my head as if in a fruit machine.' Paramedics have confirmed that similar phenomena have been described by a number of breathless women. Dr. Madra told our reporter that in one extreme case, a florid Tyneside woman had reported lust and increased libido. She told him, 'Eeh, I've never known anything like it: palpitations, sudden urges, what's the best advice?' 'Never give all the heart, Mrs. X. Never give all the heart,' he had replied.

Wallflowers

There's a wall where the lasses sit.

Age is no barrier on the wall, it's not high.
Generations of women sit there
together, as if in an old photograph,

the mother always in the middle

only moving when the ice cream van pulls up and
belts out its ear bashing version of *Match Of The Day*.

Then there's big Davey, the Dublin lad
with his steel capped boots and tan.

He's great with the kids: Caused a stir last week
when he pleaded with the lasses,
'Would wun of you at least find a man of your own?
This wun's calling me *da* and I'm not having it!'

Lasses just laughed and told him to stick
the kettle on.

Meet Billy the Brush doing his weekly sweep,
pushing his barrow as if uphill.
The kind of man who, if it rained soup would have a fork.
God love him for no one else will, except Mary

who only sits on the wall on Fridays.

Seems like everything's been tried,
to foil the vandals and keep them sweet:
youth clubs, potted plants, swings, you name it.

But they leave the wall alone.

Season after beautiful season
the lasses sit on the wall.

And Pat's arse, like a conference pear,
        loves me, loves me not, loves me, loves me not.

Band Of Hope

And Glory, when eleven visitors landed
on the street, Sunday morning.
White shirts and ebony ties
like proud, upright piano keys.
Blood-red banded, black peaked hats
completed the look. A choir of
non-rust voices announced their arrival.
And people came out.

The couple in faded blue denim:
she made no attempt to disguise
his unfaded gift above her left eye.
The man pushing a buggy with one hand
whinged that he'd fancied sleeping late,
'No bloody chance,' he snarled
at his wide awake, bouncing baby.
Single file, bike-riding children emerged
like a score of rise and fall crotchets,
teeming out from *Fat Man's Squeeze*,
the skinniest cat piss alley on the estate.
Calling out football chants, they encircled the choir
and continued to pedal around and around
like a ballsy shoal of baleful sharks.

Twin girls, blonde and red freckled
formed the front stalls, their teething sister
straddling a bony hip. Lovingly
they mopped up her pain drenched,
rosebud mouth with an off-white, flannelette bib.
Three brassed-off mothers suspended briefly
the talk on the street, then carried on *fortissimo*.
And the boy in the background, pint-size,

leaned against the notice-bearing lamp post,
'Hey Mister, are *you* the army? Mam says
her boyfriend's joined the army. Went away.
Sometimes, she goes and sees him;
catches the special bus on Saturdays.'

Scent Of A Woman

When a new love gives you
perfume for Christmas

you want to swim in it; spray it
in places you haven't touched

in years. When you discover
it's the perfume his first love wore

you want explosive sex
before spraying some in his eyes.

Orange Moon

Villanelle for a vampire

An orange moon hung low in the black sky.
How fitting, I thought, for our first date.
Pudding and pie, kiss the girls and make them cry.

There was something special about this guy.
I'd met my dreamboat, my perfect soul mate.
An orange moon hung low in the black sky.

He wore a black suit, white shirt, black tie.
When we kissed I watched his red eyes dilate.
Pudding and pie, kiss the girls and make them cry.

His slender hand stroked my virgin-white thigh.
I told him father didn't like me out late.
An orange moon hung low in the black sky.

He walked me home, I felt giddy and shy.
Like moonstruck lovers we stood at my gate.
Pudding and pie, kiss the girls and make them cry.

I slept like a baby, his bones sucked dry.
The headlines reported his cruel fate.
An orange moon hung low in the black sky.
Pudding and pie, kiss the girls and make them cry.

The Street

A black dog stands perfectly still
like a full stop at the end of the lane.

She wonders if the man at 42
still cleans his bike in the bedroom
and did his wife ever get sectioned?

Does the man at 39
still wear a wig and mime to Cilla Black?

The street still smells the same:
Newspaper, vinegar,
Mrs. Blenkinsop's warm saveloy dips,
her Max Factor lipstick, red as tomato sauce;
hair as black as the dog.

And the shop on the corner:

Dear Mrs. Fanthorpe,
small white sliced
Omo
bag of sugar
fire lighters
'til Friday.
Much obliged.

She remembers how she would wait and wait
until the shop was empty
before slipping her mother's crumpled note
across the counter, passing the time
counting love bites
on Mrs. Fanthorpe's dinosaur neck.

No talk on the street now.
NO LOITERING. NO BALL GAMES. NO FLY-TIPPING.
No skipping, no songs.

The faint sound of a bicycle bell
ting-a-lings the silence as Mr. and Mrs. 42 pedal past.
Other ghosts wave from frost flowered sash windows.
The only survivor on the street,
Mr. Brown's peachy rose bush
waiting to explode into bloom like a firework.

Northern Vowels

Steam clouds the platform like a launderette
as she looks out through the small square window,

chin resting on her cold, cupped hand,
still as a Rodin sculpture.

Well travelled passengers get on board
lugging their worn leather cases

but the journey south might as well be the moon
for she's leaving northern vowels behind her.

She'll take with her the river that made her,
a pen and a piece of coal, the tranquility of

Holy Island: *hinny, bonnie lass, kiddar.*
Feeling like a novice skydiver, she moves to

a seat by the door. She is the girl who's
keeping her coat on, breathing through a straw.

Last Waltz

Bedroom slippers are her dance shoes now,
still shining like silver paper

as we slow waltz around the kitchen.
One two   three   one

two three. Left hand resting on my shoulder,
right hand palm to palm with mine,

her wedding ring no longer round.
Without band or CD

we sing her favourite: *Moonlight and Roses.*
The mother I meet this morning

smiles as she did at nineteen, her twenty inch waist
the envy of every girl in the dance hall.

Resting her head on my breast
she whispers how much she's missed me.

Today I am my father, yesterday
her schoolgirl daughter, scolded

for not clearing my plate. The glitter ball stops
right above us; we collect our prize and pour tea.

Indigo Dreams Publishing
132, Hinckley Road
Stoney Stanton
Leicestershire
LE9 4LN
www.indigodreams.co.uk